" Working mothers, congratulate yourselves: You are not only pioneering another step in the emancipation of women and making a significant contribution to the economic well-being of your family and your country, but it is likely that your children will be well supported in their emotional and educational development by your energy and example.

This is the message given by Amita in this well researched and presented book, which is full of clear and concise advice on bringing up your children. *Working Mothers, Happy Kids* is of great value to all mothers, whether working in the home or in their careers or businesses.

We fathers must read this book too, as we need to be equally active in supporting the emotional and educational growth of our children. "

– *Ian Robertson, Managing Director, Out of the Box Thinking*

Working Mothers, Happy Kids

by Amita Dholakia

with illustrations by Mariko Jesse

BLACKSMITH BOOKS

Working Mothers, Happy Kids

I dedicate this book to my parents. I would not nurture my kids as well as I do but for the love and understanding I received from you.

BLACKSMITH BOOKS
5th Floor, 24 Hollywood Road, Central, Hong Kong
mail@blacksmithbooks.com
www.blacksmithbooks.com

ISBN-13: 978-988-99799-1-1

Copyright © 2007
Text by Amita Dholakia
Illustrations by Mariko Jesse
With thanks to Shuba

All rights reserved. No part of this publication may be reproduced, stored in a retrieval system, or transmitted in any form or by any means, electronic, mechanical, photocopying, recording or otherwise, without the prior written permission of the publisher.

Blacksmith Books fulfils mail orders for all our titles free of charge. For a free catalogue and order form, please write to us or visit our website.

Contents

1.	Seize the Moment	13
2.	Create Fun	17
3.	Banish Stress	21
4.	Share New Experiences	25
5.	Devise Secret Family Codes	29
6.	Laugh Together	33
7.	Tune In	37
8.	Plan Small Surprises	41
9.	Keep a Balance	45
10.	Communicate	49
11.	Use Others as Intermediaries	53
12.	Do Housework Together	57
13.	Maintain a High Touch Relationship	61

14.	Show Respect	65
15.	Empower your Children	71
16.	Teach by Example	77
17.	Quality Time and Discipline	81
18.	Quality Time, Learning and Development	89
19.	Make Special Dates	95
20.	Make Quality Time for Yourself	99
21.	Be Positive	103

Acknowledgements

I want to thank Anupa for strategic direction; Ma, Deta, Motima and Shaleena for feedback and encouragement; Ashish for being the best brother; and Madhabi for her views. I am genuinely grateful to Anuradha Baruah for all her help. Thanks also to Dr. Vaz, Latha and Emma. Most of all, thanks to Meghna and Vir for their cherished presence in my life.

Introduction

Liberation was meant to expand women's opportunities, not to limit them.
— Elaine Heffner

One of the most hotly discussed issues of this generation is the working mother's dilemma: to quit mid-career, giving up money, status and stimulation to look after one's children; or to continue employment and leave the nurturing to someone else.

Although some mothers are happy and confident in the choice they make to work after childbirth, many feel ambivalent about going to work and leaving their children at day care or with a childcare provider. Most feel guilty and upset about not having enough time to stimulate, discipline or love their children. Whether they work due to economic necessity, peer pressure or because it's their passion, employed mothers

are invariably burdened with questions such as:
- Will their children love them less because they are not around more?
- Will the kids be less disciplined or more prone to violent and aggressive behaviour as a result of the lack of adequate warmth they may have received?
- Will their learning and development be equal to those whose mothers stayed home?
- Will they be secure, positive, considerate, independent and socially competent individuals when they grow up?

These feelings stem from the kind of upbringing we had when we were growing up. We have memories of our mothers being around 24/7, tending to every basic need and frequently rewarding us with hot, delicious, home-cooked treats. We remember them picking us up or dropping us off at school, nursing us when we fell sick and attending our music or drama performances with regularity. We formed our parental bonds, developed our sense of values and derived our learning through the sheer quantity of time that our mothers spent with us. Our education in life was not through special experiences our parents planned for us but happened as a matter of course.

Naturally there were gaps in child-rearing then: children not being given adequate stimulation, particular interests not being encouraged, or parents being physically present and meeting the child's basic needs but not being emotionally responsive or communicative. We remember only the good things and use them as a yardstick for comparison with our lifestyle today.

The world has changed from thirty years ago. We live in a more dynamic and competitive environment. There are large numbers of employed mothers in the workforce and stronger formal support infrastructure – day care centres, nannies, babysitters and schools. Though our goal today may be the same as that of our mothers – to engender happy, secure and capable children and sustain a loving relationship with them – the means are bound to differ.

While the nurturing that our mothers did happened unceremoniously in the quantity time they spent with us, today's working mothers have to be more actively involved in their children's growth and development in the quality time they spend with their children. We learned responsibility when asked to lay the dinner table for a party of twenty; our children will learn it when we seek their active participation in household chores or empower them to make choices about their life early on. We learned about compassion and friendship when our mothers sent us with a packed lunchbox to a sick friend's house; our children will learn it at their play dates. We gained knowledge about geography and nature on our occasional family holidays; our children will acquire theirs on planned family vacations and on trips to the science centre. We participated in sports at community events; our children get special tennis coaching. Raising children in the past was more spontaneous and relaxed. Today, it is more designed and active.

Active nurturing is the reality of today and the basis of this book. For employed mothers, it refers to the spirit of the time you spend with your children in a way that will make them feel encouraged, inspired, empowered, tickled or valued. Active nurturing does not require you to fill every moment of your time with your children with intense activities, but when you are together, you should remember to be positive, warm and emotionally responsive. Active nurturing is for the mothers who need or want to work and do the best for their children. The insights in this book, along with many that you will develop from your individual experiences with your children, will empower you to enrich your lives together.

Note: For the purpose of this book, 'work' has been used to mean employment for income.

Insight 1
Seize the Moment

Know what's most important and give it all you've got

As working mothers, most of our day is spent doing chores, office work or caring for the kids. Spending quality time with our partners or friends means having moments alone with them to talk or do things together. When it comes to children, however, we forget that to spend quality time means to be with them one-on-one without any distractions.

We all know mothers who take their children to parks or restaurants only to spend all their time talking on the phone; or who go to social events where they chat with friends while the children must amuse themselves. I am guilty of the same. Temporarily a stay-at-home mother, I don't deceive myself that just because I have a lot of time with my daughter necessarily implies that I am building stronger bonds with her than if I were out working in an office. There are occasions when I am cooking or reading a newspaper while occasionally intervening in her play. I find myself saying "Where is your play dough, honey?" or "Why don't you put on a new dress for your doll?" while my attention is really focused on whether the vegetables are cooked or if I have read through the lifestyle section of the paper. I can clearly see her looking a little forlorn because she can sense that my two bits of conversation is patronising and intended to dismiss her to do her own thing while I do mine.

Although not all the time that you spend with your child will be exclusive, seize the moments that can be. Try to ensure you give her undivided attention for at least one hour in the day: talking to her, participating in her games, letting her take the lead without talking on the phone, working on your presentation or having friends come over.

See your child's face light up when you drop everything just to be with her. Multi-tasking applies to office and home chores, not to time with your children.

Insight 2
Create Fun

Have fun in what you are doing and you shall succeed

Asked to recall the happiest memories of childhood in a recent study, many adults talked about their family vacations, singing with siblings in the back of the car while taking a drive, or visiting relatives at festivals. The unpleasant memories comprised being nagged by parents or being forced to fulfil parental aspirations. The happy times were associated with the FUN moments the family spent together, while the not-so-happy memories involved pressure and expectations.

FUN is a key ingredient to forge strong bonds with children. In a family setup where the father is employed and the mother stays home to look after the kids, a lot of the mother's time is spent feeding, bathing and disciplining them. Fathers, on the other hand, come home from work and focus mostly on spending FUN time with the children – playing games, reading them stories or taking them out. That's perhaps why, even though stay-at-home mothers may spend three times the number of hours that working fathers spend with their children, the kids usually show equal affection for both parents.

For mothers employed full-time, it is okay to delegate the routine tasks of child rearing to a caregiver as long as you remember to schedule fun activities in your weekly calendar. Go to the park on the weekend, do finger painting with your kids or go for a ride in the car with lots of cool music to sing along to.

Enjoy your children fully when they are with you and they will cherish the time you spend together.

now what shall we call our family masterpiece ?
happy mess!
together mess!

Insight 3
Banish Stress

Make home surroundings pleasant for your children

No matter what your type of work or personality – hyper, inflexible or collected – if you are serious about spending quality time with your children then you should avoid getting stressed when you are with them.

This is natural enough. Having an anxious or tense person around can spoil everyone's spirits. A caregiver's mood swings can be detrimental to the feeling of security and self esteem in children.

I know a mother of two kids who is constantly on edge. She wants to be a perfect mother with perfect children who do well academically as well as in sports and drama. She wants her house neat and clean, her home-cooked meals nutritious and wholesome and her office work faultless. She is continuously stressed striving to meet her own expectations and keeps passing on the stress to her children – shouting at, chiding or pressurising them. The result: the children try to avoid their mother and would rather spend time with dad, who is calmer and more relaxed.

Juggling multiple responsibilities of household, children and employment can give anyone frazzled nerves. You can either fret over issues that cannot be solved by worrying about them, and in the process end up making yourself and your children unhappy; or resolve that when it comes to your children you will not let stress get in the way of your relationship and time with them.

As we all naturally gravitate towards individuals who are unruffled and cool, children too would prefer to spend time with unstressed, relaxed mothers.

When things get really bad, remember your long-term goal: to raise your children to be affectionate, happy, secure individuals. Keep repeating the mantra "Happy mums make happy kids".

Insight 4
Share New Experiences

Rediscover the world with your child

When couples want to spend quality time with each other, they might take walks together or set a dinner date. When they want to spend really special time with each other, they go away on holiday.

Why is it that taking a break and spending quality time for couples (whether they have kids or not) typically involves going to places away from home?

It's because being in a different place means being far from the monotony of work, daily chores (planning the day, cooking, cleaning), children's demands and social pressures. More importantly, being out and away offers new and exciting experiences.

It's the same for kids. The older ones have some pressures to escape – parental demands to do well in academic and extra-curricular activities, multiple classes to attend, homework and peer anxiety. For toddlers, it is the humdrum of daily existence.

Taking the kids elsewhere is a break from their everyday loads, but it's also something else: when you get out of the house and explore the world, you are immersed in new experiences together. Over a period these collected novel occurrences become the "things you did together", times to reminisce about and build fond memories around.

In your daily lives, once every three months you can schedule a trip to the museum or a trek up a mountain, and once a year to an exciting, new holiday destination. Take lots of pictures and put them up in the house as a reminder to your kids of the enjoyable times that you shared.

Insight 5
Devise Secret Family Codes

Who says love speaks only one language?

We see it on screen all the time: fathers doing a 'thumbs up' with daughters after getting off a plane, or a long-separated mother and adult son showing solidarity through a unique hi-five action they had created and shared when the son was a small boy.

I know a mother who regularly uses distinct small actions – unique thumbs up or a two-line song that she and her son made together – when the son crosses a challenging obstacle or after they solve a problem. And I can see the envy of other moms as they witness this unique bond that the mother and son share to the exclusion of everything around them.

Lo-fives, hi-fives, thumbs up, your family song and dance routine or any other sign that you and your family exchange with one another can be sources of great familial bonding.

That is because you have created a special language unique to your family with secret codes meant to convey your love for each other, to say "great job" or foster a "we are a team" feeling. Such special codes can be used to soothe a crying child, distract a temper tantrum or appease a bad mood.

How wonderful it is to have these exclusive family expressions that do not take up too much time or effort, yet are a symbol of the strong bond you share.

So begin today. Create your magic family codes in as many different forms as you like, to suit different moods, and see these help foster a special connection.

Insight 6
Laugh Together

Love means sharing a laugh

How many times a day do you share a laugh with your children? It depends on the situation, you might say. There are some days you get a few laughs and then days go by without an opportunity. One cannot really create laughing situations, right?

Wrong! From Mumbai to Singapore, laughing clubs are common across Asia. Anyone can join in, irrespective of gender, age, nationality, religion or social status. All you need to join the club is heartiness of spirit and a proclivity to laugh. The members meet regularly at public parks and simply laugh for about half an hour. It begins with forced laughter from all, but merely watching so many people laugh can turn one's own effort into a completely natural and hearty endeavour. Laughing is remarkably therapeutic. It lifts the mood and promotes energy and vitality of spirit. And it costs nothing!

Some spontaneous laughter is related to specific situations, like if you slip on a wet floor and fall headlong into a bucket (without hurting yourself) or if by chance someone mispronounces your child's name. Then there is instinctive, collective laughter, and what a good feeling that is! Isn't it magical when you and your child laugh together and forget the world and your worries for those few seconds? If, in that one instant, you can capture so much energy and closeness of the bond that you and your child share, then why wait for fate to intervene with a funny situation before you share a laugh?

Create your own funny games or situations so that you can share at least one laugh a day. You can play grab each other, tickle time or dance together with your toddler on your lap with lots of jiggling and jumping. If you just keep yourself alert to laughing opportunities you will find that children laugh quite easily. It is the easiest and quickest way to connect, lighten the mood and create a cheery atmosphere.

Insight 7
Tune In

If you want understanding, try giving some

Name the following:
- Two of your child's closest friends
- Their favourite activity
- Their biggest fear
- Their worst time of the day
- Their best time of the day
- Their favourite item of clothing
- Their favourite cartoon character
- Describe their schedule at school

If you can answer six or more of these questions accurately then you are to be congratulated on being completely tuned in to your child, and you can skip this chapter. If not, then this section may help you become aware of the benefits of knowing your children well.

While spending time with our children, we often tend to concentrate on tasks at hand. When feeding them, we focus on whether they are eating their veggies or if they have finished their food. When bathing them, we just want to ensure that the task is completed successfully, from making them agree to a bath to getting dressed. Because time is short and there are always umpteen tasks to get done, we usually respond to our children in a habitual manner based on our prejudices and schedule. As a result, we forget to think of or understand their temperament, needs or likes.

However, knowing and understanding your children can help you to minimise the daily struggle of achieving routine tasks.

At bath time, Lily lets her daughter Siam take her favourite doll to the tub. So while she goes through the routine of disrobing Siam and settling her in the bath, Siam does the same with her doll. On other days, when the doll trick does not work, she tempts Siam to the bath with a tub full of bubbles and a story about sharks and turtles. Knowing her well, she uses different strategies specifically tailored to her daughter to accomplish daily tasks with minimum resistance.

If your child's worst time of the day is after school, because she is tired and hungry, it is important that she has her meal and gets a short nap even though you may want to break her out of the siesta habit. If she is at her most energetic in the afternoon, you can schedule swimming classes or outdoor playtime for her. If she gets impatient on a road trip, you can surprise her with a new toy of her favourite cartoon character that you were hiding in your bag.

You can allay your children's fears, distract them from tantrums or make them happy when you are in tune with them. Knowing your children well helps you to respond more effectively.

Insight 8
Plan Small Surprises

Pleasant surprises are moments of happiness we enjoy unprepared

The gift industry thrives on this.

Surprise your beloved on Valentine's Day! Send your mother a 'Happy Mother's Day' greeting. From birthday to bar mitzvah, graduation to get well gifts, giving a surprise is a fundamental element of expressing your love or friendship.

We all love nice surprises, and kids even more so. Surprising your kids with new toys is of course likely to make you very popular with them, but we are not talking about showering them with expensive gifts (too much of which could spoil the children) but finding ways to make them feel special.

There are lots of inexpensive little ways of doing that.

When they are toddlers, saying "I have a surprise for you" is a sure way to get their attention. You can reintroduce old toys that you have put away for a while and still generate interest if you announce them as a "surprise". As the children grow, you could occasionally get them a little something from your workplace – a handmade card, an office pen or an unneeded mouse pad, or a print of a different smiley cartoon character every Tuesday and Thursday.

Mothers who are self-employed or work from home could bring back a different type of flower or leaf from their walks or make paper stickers and bring back a new sticker with a message after every outing.

Your kids will look forward to your return from your office or from your walk. Surprises are a way of making them feel important, showing that they were in your thoughts all the while you were away from them, and that you love them.

Insight 9
Keep a Balance

The contentment of life comes not from intensity but from rhythm and harmony

In order to do the best for their children, many mothers focus excessively on the child's mental, emotional and social development. This may lead to the child pulling away or being over-indulged.

Mothers who work outside the home tend to feel guilty about having so little time with their children and often try to make up by spending intensely involved time with them. They enrol them into multiple classes outside school and try to fill their every moment with stimulating activities.

Research suggests that from a child's perspective, it doesn't matter if you work or not. What is important is that you don't feel guilty about the choice you make and manifest the stress of it in the amount of focus you place on them.

Children need relaxed hang-around time as well as intense involvement time with their parents. Not all the time they spend with you can be perfectly tailored quality time. Just 'being there emotionally' – understanding, communicating, tuning in – is important; not necessarily the number of hours you spend with them.

Balance is the key to spending quality time with your children. Just as adults need their own space, so do kids. Too much focus on the child can be as counter-productive as too little. Come to terms with your work/life anxiety and stop trying too hard to make up.

Insight 10
Communicate

Communication leads to understanding and shared values

Across the world, the single largest reason why marriages fail is communication breakdown. This happens when the partners stop speaking or listening to each other. Sometimes they either fail to acknowledge the other person's feelings or have too little time to spend with one another.

Just as strong communication is the cornerstone of a happy, successful marriage, being open, honest and communicative is the foundation of building a deep, lasting bond with your child.

Communicating with your child means not only talking and guiding her through the maze of her world and growing-up years but also really listening to her, understanding and acknowledging her feelings.

Communication also means taking a genuine interest in her world. Find some time every day to have a casual conversation about her life and yours. You can do a happy/sad bedtime routine (your prime connection time when both of you are finished with the day's activities) where you share your greatest and not-so-great moments of the day.

Encourage your child. Build her self-esteem. Observe her actions and look for ways to genuinely praise her as much as possible. Try to avoid criticising. Any child who fears being put down by the parent is unlikely to open up to that person.

Find out about the influences that affect your child in her world. Educate yourself about peer pressure, drugs, alcohol etc. Being a step ahead will help you guide her to live a safe life. You will also understand more of what she is saying when she needs to discuss these issues with you.

Most importantly, let her know that you will love and support her no matter what happens, time and again, so she knows that you care and that she has you to talk to always.

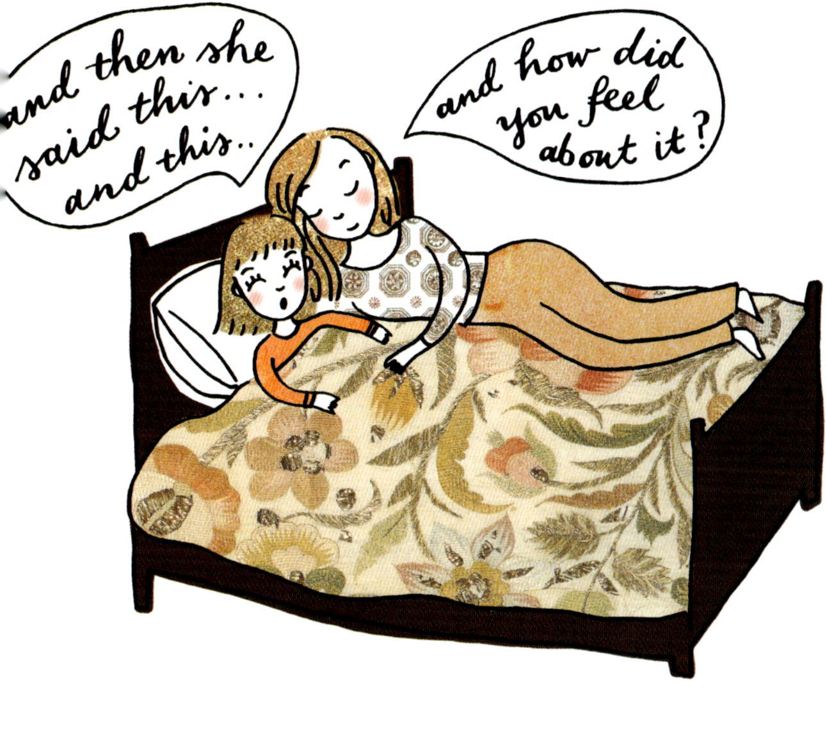
and then she said this... and this...
and how did you feel about it?

Insight 11
Use Others as Intermediaries

Don't limit a child to your own learning, for he was born in another time

Spending quality time with your child is supposed to bring you closer together. And yet, you can achieve the same result by being not the principal participant in that time but by using others to show that you care. It may sound ironic but it is possible if you can be in some way instrumental to your child feeling special, important or loved.

As your child grows older, his friends become increasingly important. He wants to spend as much time with them as possible and becomes sensitive to his friends' or peer group's inclinations and his own status amongst them.

If there is any way you can make him happy by providing an

opportunity to enjoy himself with his friends, that is another special way of building a rapport with your child.

Instead of waiting for him to ask, what if you were to invite all his friends for a sleepover or a meal over the weekend; or organise a special treat for them at his favourite restaurant; or buy them tickets to the premiere of the movie they have all been looking forward to.

If done occasionally and not often, as a substitute for your time with your child, it can be a source of great joy. It would enhance his relationship with his friends and make him feel important amongst them.

You can demonstrate your thoughtfulness by encouraging special interests that your children have. If he likes rock climbing you could sign him up for a rock climbing camp; if he likes art, you could send him to an art school. In both instances, you display an understanding of what your children like and provide them with opportunities for enhancing their self-worth.

Insight 12
Do Housework Together

Light is the task when many share the toil.
– Homer, The Iliad

If you do not have home help, you may be spending on average at least 3.5 hours a day on household chores. This means that if you live up to 75 years of age, not counting the first 18 years and the last five, you will have spent one tenth of your life doing work that is necessary but hardly thought-provoking, meaningful or productive to you. Here the reference is not to those lucky few who enjoy work for the sake of it and find purpose in everything they do, but the multitude who get tired just thinking about toiling away at what they perceive to be routine tasks.

When you know there is no way out, try to make your life a little more productive by seeking your child's participation in regular chores. Sure, a toddler is likely to slow you down when you want to go grocery shopping by wanting to examine each item on the shelves, or by spilling the jug of water when laying the table. But if you decide not to get weighed down just thinking about the damage she will do if you engage her in your chores, and instead actively enlist her help, the benefits will far outweigh the cost.

For one, unless responsibility is given, the child cannot learn to carry it out. Giving your child simple tasks to do, such as putting out the plates before dinner when she is four, locating a brand of cereal in the grocery store when she is six or asking her to bake a simple sponge cake (under supervision) for your home party when she is ten, builds her self-confidence and makes her feel important. It signals to your child that you believe in her ability to carry out the task successfully, strengthening her capacity to solve her own problems in the future.

Second, contrary to what you think, children find some household chores very pleasurable. Washing the car and baking can be great fun. But even routine tasks imbued with responsibility and a little variety (different tasks for each day of the week, for example) can be enjoyable for children. Sometimes you can augment this fun by introducing little exciting treats, like going off for ice creams or a drive in the car after completing all the chores of the day.

Third, when you get home weary from work, instead of running around doing everything yourself and reprimanding your children, you can have a regular routine with selected tasks assigned to each child. Having a certain constancy and rhythm in your life, with each member participating and doing their fair share, can be a source of great bonding for a family.

Just as having someone to share life's burdens with makes you better equipped to handle them, you will feel stronger and closer to your children for having them share in your everyday work.

Insight 13
Maintain a High Touch Relationship

Sometimes it's better to put love into hugs than into words

Science tells us that human touch produces positive effects within the body via chemicals in the brain. More powerful than morphine, these endorphins produce a sense of relaxation and wellbeing in the recipient. Moreover, if the touch comes from someone with whom there is a positive bond, like a mother, there is a feeling of heightened love and security.

In a recent report that appeared in a Manila newspaper, about 15 of the 70-100 children born annually in a city hospital are premature or have a low birthweight. There are only 14 incubators in the hospital, and since the weakest children need several days' stay, incubator space is at a premium. With no money to buy new incubators, the hospital five years ago began using the 'Kangaroo Mother Care' method that involves putting only the very weakest babies in mechanical incubators and swaddling the rest with their mothers. Since the programme was adopted, the Manila hospital has seen a dramatic 30 percent fall in deaths among low birthweight babies. According to a head doctor at the hospital, "The babies' heartbeat and temperature remain much more stable when they are with their mothers, and they tend to gain weight faster and go home a lot quicker than those in incubators". It is obvious that a mother's continuous physical embrace gives her child adequate warmth and strength for survival.

In the first few years, the mother's touch is known to have a profound effect not only on physical development but also on the child's emotional growth and social abilities. Studies done by James W. Prescott, a research scientist at the American National Institute of Child Health, in the mid-1970s established that deprivation of touch early in life could cause depression, social withdrawal and a lack of empathy in a child. On the other hand, children who receive adequate physical affection are likely to be more compassionate, trusting and emotionally secure.

Recent studies further suggest that a mother's affectionate interactions with her child promote intellectual development.

With your touch, you have a special power to influence your child's physical, emotional and mental wellbeing in his early years. Use this power abundantly. Make your child feel loved, nurtured, safe and secure in his environment. Be free with cuddles and kisses. Make a simple hug a part of your daily ritual. Encourage with a pat on the back; soothe with a head massage; make up with a kiss. Be conscious of the impact of touch and conscientious of its necessity.

Insight 14
Show Respect

Give respect to get it

As adults, we recognise appropriate social behaviour. Our children have to learn it. We can practise self-control. Our children must be trained to do it. We understand the distinction between safe and harmful. Our children have to be told about it. Because of the huge gap between all that we are aware of and understand and what our children know, we tend to treat them as little babies who must listen to us, mind their behaviour and be grateful to us for all that we are doing for them. And we feel wretched when our children misbehave, defy orders or show ingratitude.

But next time, before you feel irritated by your child's behaviour, reflect a little on yours. When you ask her to do something, is your tone commanding or courteous? When she misbehaves, do you react immediately or first try to understand the reason for it?

The tone and manner of your responses to your child's actions are likely to have a fundamental influence on your child's demeanour towards you and others.

Here are two mother-child interactions that make the point:

Example 1

Boy: "Mum, I'm afraid of the dark."

Mother's obvious response: "There is no need to be scared. You are a big boy now. You have to learn to sleep in the dark."

Mother's empathetic response: "It is dark because it is night time, and night is for sleeping. Do you want me to put on a night light for you?"

In the first response the child's fear is handled with relative disregard; in the second, it is treated with respect and the mother provides both a reason and an aid to help the child cope.

<u>Example 2</u>

Girl: "Mum, I want a sweet now."

Mother's obvious response: "You can't have another. You have had two already. No more."

Mother's empathetic response: "Do you know what happens if you eat too many sweets? Your teeth will decay and become painful. Then you will have go to the dentist. Do you want to go to the dentist?"

Here again, the first response is standard. Naturally, the request for a third sweet cannot be entertained. But as the empathetic response suggests, the mother can respond to the girl's demand in a considerate manner by offering an explanation.

This insight does not suggest that providing explanations will solve all your problems. For example, in the above case, the verbal exchange between child and mother may not end there. The child may say "Yes, I want to go to the dentist" or not listen and whine to have another sweet. The idea is to be conscious of the child's need for dignity and respect and to practise this in your responses to them.

Though small in size, children are independent beings. They want to be treated with respect and not as mere things. They don't want you to be dismissive of their fears, needs or desires. If you disagree with them, they want you to be patient enough to explain and tell them why.

You will receive respect from them if you choose to give them the same.

I want to take my teddy bear to the beach
How about we take your spade and give your teddy bear a rest today, so he can be happy to see you when you get back.

Insight 15
Empower your Children

Give your children problems to solve, not answers to remember

Here's the story of a marketing professional who has worked for two Fortune 500 corporations in her career.

The first company she worked for was characterized by tight central control from its headquarters in New York. As employees in Asia, her team was expected merely to follow and execute commands relayed down to them on how to market products in Asia. It did not seem to matter that, being closer to the consumers than senior management in the United States, they understood native needs and usage more and were in a better position to develop local strategies.

Being a mere pawn, following orders that she did not always agree with and unable to use either her creativity or market understanding was a frustrating experience. It was her first job; she did not know any better and so she spent five trying years there.

The second company she worked for was strikingly different from the first. Though they had their head office in the UK and she was in Asia, they gave her autonomy and flexibility. The rewards were based on her performance. Her performance was dependent entirely on her efforts, market understanding and the strategic decisions that she made in her work. She felt motivated and challenged. Her second company believed in her, and so she felt treasured and empowered.

This illustrates a universal truth. No one likes being continuously told what to do. Individuals like to exercise their views and feel they are being heard.

You will have faced such challenges several times in your life. What do you feel when you are given a sermon at work by your boss on how to improve in your job, or given continuous advice by peers or parents on how to bring up children? Resentment, anger, helplessness!

Your child is no different. While she is dependent upon you to teach her life skills, she feels helpless in face of the power you have over her. As she grows and becomes conscious of her own personality, she feels the need to assert her independence.

Continuous control by the parent over how the child should function can be frustrating. Just think of the stream of advice that we dish out each day:

"Let me open that jar for you, Sonia."

"It's bedtime now."

"It's bathtime now."

"That is not a party dress, wear the pink one."

We need to extend freedom to our children in such a way that they do not become out of control.

Fortunately, there are ways in which you can encourage autonomy. Here are some specific ideas.

- Give your children alternatives. Widen the scope as they grow older. You can ask a toddler whether he would like rice or pasta for dinner. An older child can be asked whether he would like his birthday party at the park or at home.

- Do not rush in to offer solutions to a problem. Encourage them to figure it out. If your child is unable to complete a jigsaw puzzle, give her a hint of where a piece might fit.
- Do not suppress their hopes. Don't say things like, "You can never be a doctor. Doctors have to keep their rooms clean and tidy. You are so messy."
- Don't ask too many questions. Don't say, "Where were you?", "Why are you so dirty?", "What happened at the party?" and so on. Constant monitoring can make the child feel stifled.
- Don't be over-involved. Continuously brushing your daughter's hair, straightening her dress, or getting involved in microscopic details of her life – from how she wants to spend her pocket money to what kind of card she wants to make for her friend – is likely to make her feel distressed.

By gradually relaxing your hold on your child as she grows, you will help her to become independent and function in the future without you. At the same time, she will respect you for respecting her space.

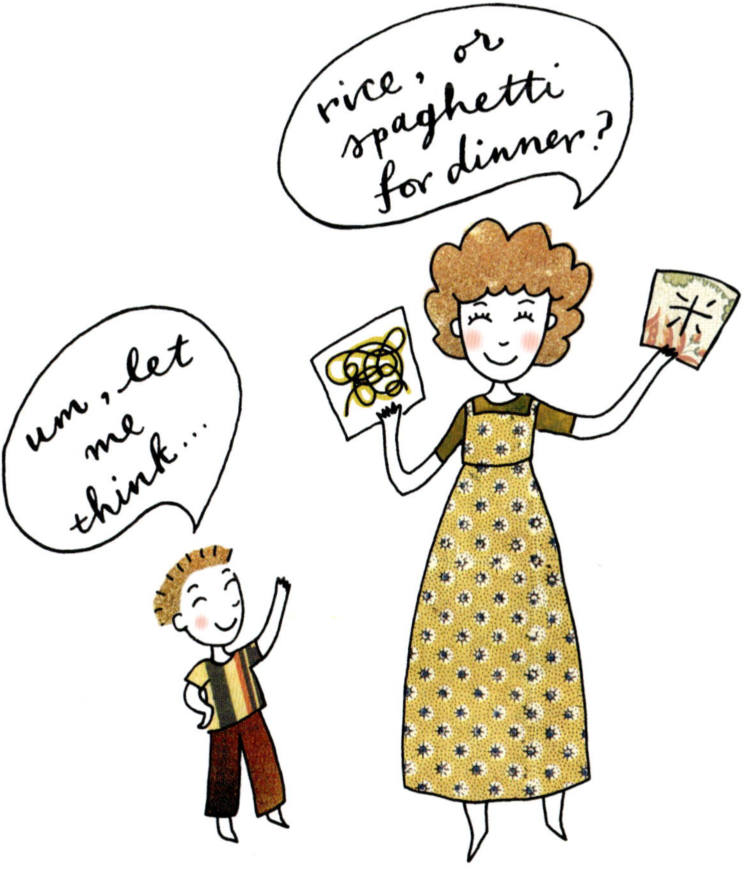
rice, or spaghetti for dinner?
um, let me think...

Insight 16
Teach by Example

I watched my father live; and learned how

The most important insight for actively nurturing your kids is to bear in mind that children learn what they live.

Recently, a story appeared in a business magazine about a French-born Muslim boy who had to endure taunts of "Go back to your country, Arab" from his non-Muslim schoolmates. How demoralising! Children aren't born partisan but they see the way the adults around them respond to those of a different race, religion or sexual orientation, and follow the same course. But just as they can learn intolerance or hostility, children can also learn compassion and acceptance. The best way to raise open-minded, considerate and loving children is by example.

If you ban discriminatory comments in your house and welcome diversity, your children will grow up capable of living in a multicultural world. If you treat persons less fortunate than yourself with equal regard as you do your peers, your children are likely to turn out respectful and considerate of others, irrespective of their stature or wealth.

Even in daily life, children tend to imitate their parents' behaviour and attitude on a smaller scale. Although you may gain immense gratification when your children reflect your words and actions, it is a good time for you to think about practising the conduct you would like to see in your children. I have learned to speak softly since my daughter turned two and started making her requests known in a loud tone, the way I used to. On the plus side, I feel happy when she shows her affection with warm embraces and "I love you" intonations because that's the way I have raised her.

Every day, you have conscious choices to make when it comes to responding to your children. Often, those choices are between good, helpful, thoughtful and rational responses, and bad, hurtful, thoughtless and unreasonable responses. If you espouse criticism, your children will learn to condemn; if you exercise praise, they will learn to appreciate. The best gift you can give is to lead by example.

Insight 17
Quality Time and Discipline

Discipline requires mutual respect and trust

Quality time and discipline. To many parents, these are opposing concepts. The first is based on sharing warm moments to create strong bonds with your child; and the second on using a firm hand to teach appropriate behaviour. Can the twain ever meet?

They can. They come together in an idea called 'positive discipline'. The purpose of positive discipline is to promote the development of life skills and respectful relationships in family, school, business and community systems. It essentially works on the principle that if disciplining has to work, it requires mutual respect and trust, not external control over a person by force or intimidation.

Although your child's temperament, your parenting style and the situation will all influence the methods you use, it is important to know the tools used for positive discipline. Armed with these you can employ the same spirit of warmth, openness and understanding in disciplining as you would for active nurturing. Effective positive discipline combines both proactive and responsive tools to teach a child appropriate behaviour.

The following list of proactive tools with examples each is a good start to enforcing positive discipline in your home.

- **Avoid a build-up to conflict**

Keep your precious items out of reach of small children. This will help you to avoid power struggles arising from your child touching your valuables.

- **Establish routines**

This helps children to understand what follows each task. A lack of routines can unsettle children and make them cranky.

- **Ensure a safe environment**

Plug a child brace into the power sockets instead of running after your child saying "No" every time he wants to check out the light switch.

- **Plan proactively**

On long car trips, carry enough activity material to keep children busy.

- **Teach by example**

If your manner is polite and considerate towards others, theirs will be too.

- **Choose your battles**

Set a few non-negotiable rules that you feel most strongly about, and stick to them. Give in for other situations. You may want to strongly reprimand your child if he is rude towards another person. But if you are working in your study and your child needs you, perhaps you can be less strict.

If you can be accommodating some of the time, your child will feel less pressured to assert himself in all situations.

Responsive tools are required in situations which cannot be planned for. Use these depending on the situation.

- **Distract**

Because of their short attention spans, younger children can easily be distracted from potentially harmful or annoying activities. If your daughter wants the toy that her brother has, distract her by offering something different: another toy or a game of hide and seek.

• **Redirect behaviour**

Give children acceptable alternatives to what they want to do. Your son may not be permitted to paint on the walls, but you can give him a piece of paper or fabric on which he can exercise his imagination.

• **Use reasoning**

Explaining the reason for a particular action helps the child to learn right from wrong. For example, instead of using force or threats, you can say "If you don't wash your hands after play, you'll get germs and you might get sick."

• **Give limited tasks**

Asking a child to clear up the mess after a finger painting session may seem overwhelming to him. It is more effective to allocate limited tasks, such as putting the colours back into the box, and help with the rest.

• **Forewarn**

I have had great success using this approach. Instead of inflicting an order on the child, forewarn her. She will feel more respected and less compelled to resist. Instead of saying "It's time for your bath, come along now", you can say "You have five minutes to finish playing, and then we will have a bath so that you can be all clean and fresh for bed."

- **Use positive language**

Numerous studies suggest that children co-operate with parents more readily if directives are communicated in a positive language rather than by commanding, chiding or threatening to withdraw love. It is more effective to say "Your room needs cleaning, do you need help?" rather than "I won't speak to you unless you clean your room" or "You are so messy. Get your room cleaned now."

- **Make the child conscious of the feelings of others**

Making the child understand the effect of his actions on others is likely to instil a sense of consideration in him. Saying "It's painful when you hit me" or "I don't like getting pinched, it hurts" is more effective than hitting back or accusing the child of being bad. It will allow him to understand the consequences of his action and the reason to refrain from it in future.

- **Allow consequences**

Children should be allowed to make some mistakes and learn from them. Throwing a toy out of the window will only mean that your child cannot play with it any more.

- **Teach problem-solving**

This technique applies to older kids who can respond effectively to questions posed to them. It involves encouraging children to think of solutions to disciplinary issues. This fulfils their need for autonomy and promotes independent thinking. Thinking first, instead of acting on impulse, also helps children to become less emotional when frustrated.

I recall two cases in which mothers used problem-solving to come up with answers to their children troubles. In the first case, a girl was always undoing her seat belt while in a moving car. When the mother asked her how she could make her sit without taking the seat belt off, the child said she wanted her mum to play her favourite CDs while driving, so she could hum along to them. In the other case, a boy always wanted to sit in the shopping cart at the supermarket and eat food from the shelves. The mother started to carry grapes when she went to the store with her son, to distract him from the boxes of cereals and sweets.

- **Build on success**

Reinforce good behaviour. It will make your child feel self-confident and understand appropriate personal and social manners. Be specific in your praise. Instead of saying, "You are a good girl, Tanya," say, "You put back your toys and books. That was a very responsible thing to do. It's nice to see a clean room, Tanya."

These positive techniques will help you practise teaching your child the right life skills without resorting to punishment or withdrawing your attention.

No matter how difficult your child, providing a warm, loving environment and practising a nurturing but firm style of discipline will make your child emotionally secure.

Insight 18
Quality Time, Learning and Development

When the fun goes out of play, so does the learning

Just as limbs develop greater flexibility and tone if stretched often, brain cells gain strength when exercised regularly. The more you stimulate your child's brain, the greater his capacity to grow, learn and adapt to an ever-changing world.

According to Maria Montessori, one of the world's greatest educators, "The early years of life are the most important years of a child's growth, when unconscious learning gradually emerges to the conscious level." Children possess an unusual sensitivity and intellectual ability, unlike adults, to absorb and learn from their environment, both in quality and quantity. There are sensitive periods of a child's development: periods when the child seeks certain stimuli with immense intensity and, consequently, can most easily master a particular skill. For example, a child of early years is capable of becoming proficient in several languages.

In addition to love and understanding, you need to provide appropriate training to help develop your child's mental, physical and social skills relative to his ability. Here's how you can create a challenging learning environment.

Encourage play

Play is the single most critical tool for natural learning. It allows children to take risks without fear of failure. It builds confidence as children experiment and master different tasks, stimulates problem-solving and promotes imaginative thinking. Create a pleasant atmosphere for your child to play in. Earmark a play area where he can play without fear of too many limits. Collect toys and games which are safe, non-violent, suited to his temperament, and which encourage creative and cognitive abilities.

Participate

Playing a game together or reading a story to your child is an invaluable way to bond. Schedule some time each day for involved play, reading or story time.

Be prepared

Children don't wait. For a special activity like cooking or art, gather all the materials before involving your child.

Get ideas from others

The primary method of learning childcare in olden times was by meeting and communicating with other mothers. Seize the opportunity when presented to you, or do it the 21st century way, i.e. online. Amazon.com has mothers and experts who provide information on the most suitable toys and books for different age groups. There are lots of parenting websites with tons of information on child learning and development issues. Scour sites to find the information you are looking for. Getting different perspectives on a specific aspect of child rearing will help you form your own.

Choose a suitable school

If possible, make personal visits to a few schools on your shortlist. Talk to the teachers. Sit through a class. Understand the curriculum and the teaching philosophy. Check out the facilities and the environment. Select a school that meets your education expectations and where your child will be happy.

Exploit new learning opportunities

Active nurturing requires that you are constantly conscious of your child's developmental needs and provide apt stimulus for them. Take reading, for example. At six months your child is ready to be read bright and colourful pop-up or feel-and-learn books. At one year, books with pictures of identifiable objects such as animals can be read. At two years, concepts of colours, shapes and numbers may be introduced. Between the ages of two and three, your child enters the fascinating world of stories. There are books, videos, TV programmes and toys available for every age and every aspect of a child's intellectual and social growth. Cartoons, animal shows, discovery and science centres, museums, parks and playgroups provide ample opportunities for getting to know new things about the world around us. Keeping yourself open to these will help you create a rich learning experience for your child every step of the way.

Insight 19
Make Special Dates

Personalized attention to someone means treating him or her with value

It's the weekend. He wants to go swimming; she wants to go on slides and rides in the park. He wants to eat burgers and fries; she is clamouring for doughnuts or dim sum. They both want to watch different programmes on TV at the same time. The conflict is endless.

They are two different personalities, often two different genders, with contrasting needs, likes and responses. And they have one mother. You would like to give more of yourself to each of them but you have to divide your love and attention equally. You cannot please them both completely in the same instant. So you try to balance their interests so that sometimes, one's will prevails for a while, and then the other will have her say. More often than not, you resolve the conflict by proposing a compromise.

Through this balance and adjustment, children learn to share and wait for their turn. They learn to live as a family, in a close group of people who love each other, do fun things together and often get into fights.

Filial happiness, shared love and family activities are an integral part of people's lives. However, human beings are also individuals who need personal attention and fulfilment of their needs and aspirations.

While they derive great joy (and pain!) from sibling ties, your children also want you to interact with them one-on-one. As young self-seeking people, they want to be exclusively appreciated for their good qualities, listened to for their views and encouraged in their positive pursuits.

When you make special time for your child, it helps you develop a better understanding of him or her. It demonstrates your recognition of their unique importance in your life, thereby forging a particular closeness.

As a bonus, studies have shown that spending one-on-one time and valuing the individuality of each child actually promotes better sibling relationships!

Sonia has two young children: three-year-old Sara and six-month-old Neil. She recently underwent a harrowing experience when her son was admitted to hospital with a lung infection. For four days, she stayed with Neil while her husband looked after Sara. By the fourth day, Neil was happy and healthy, and came home. Sonia then decided to devote some time exclusively to Sara, as she had not spent much time with her in the previous four days. For two hours, they played Sara's favourite music, danced, read three books and played a cooking game. In that time, both Sara and Sonia laughed a lot. At the end of the two hours Sara looked radiant and happy and Sonia got a big hug and a kiss. More importantly for Sonia, it was a moment when she felt a deep intimacy with her daughter.

Children, whether they are younger or older, do sometimes want exclusive attention from you. It's great when you do things as a family. But don't forget to make special dates with your child to acknowledge him or her as a unique individual.

OK, go to your boring girl's party, Sara! Tomorrow, mum's mine! We're going to Dino Park for burgers!
bye honey! we'll be back soon!

Insight 20
Make Quality Time for Yourself

The time to relax is when you don't have time for it

Mothers with little time and lots to do think it is selfish and indulgent to take time out to develop a self-care routine. Yet there is a certain amount of attention needed in order to be an effective mother and person.

One of the most important things is your health. Good health equips you with the necessary physical energy and mental stamina to cope with life's demands. You need to look after your body, eat a healthy diet, get regular exercise and enough sleep, and go for regular medical checkups.

The mind matters too. All of us feel torn on a daily basis – trying to raise our children in the best way possible while struggling to maintain a separate identity. But unless there is personal development, we tend to stagnate and our sense of self-worth diminishes. So, no matter what it takes, whether it is work that presents the opportunity for intellectual growth or a hobby – gardening, painting or tennis – be sure to find time away from your daily hullabaloo to nourish your mind.

The soul, like the body and the mind, lives by what it feeds on. You need love, excitement and rest as much as your children. Instead of merely preaching to your children the benefit of nurturing their souls, be a good example to them and make time for yours. Read a book, go shopping, get a manicure or have a heart-to-heart with a girlfriend.

The most important thing you can give your family is your happiness and peace of mind. That can happen only when you feel fulfilled and your mind, body and spirit are taken care of.

Insight 21
Be Positive

Our happiness depends more on our attitudes than on our circumstances

There are three primary factors for employed mothers feeling dejected and negative.

The first is guilt, which springs from the conflict between the way we believe life should be and the way it is. For generations we have been taught that the primary responsibility for childcare rests with the mother. When we go to work and delegate a large part of that responsibility to someone else, that age-old belief bothers us. We frequently question our reasons for being employed and feel guilty about not being around enough to nurture our children. The feeling is exacerbated when others – our mothers or friends – try to impose their contrary expectations on us, or in unanticipated instances like when the child is sick.

The second is the weight of overwhelming work to be accomplished. For mothers who work in high-pressure jobs and have little support, managing home, children and work can be onerous and tiring.

The third trigger for feeling down is not finding enough time to take care of one's own needs, like exercise or relaxation.

As an employed mother, all the above are part of your life and are bound to affect you. Sure enough, you can wallow in your wretchedness occasionally, voice your frustrations to a girlfriend or sit in a corner and mope. However, it is a good idea to keep this feeling localised to the event that has triggered it, and ensure it does not develop into chronic negative behaviour.

The reason is obvious. Your negativity has a direct impact on your child's sense of self-worth. If you are often stressed out, they will want to avoid you; if you are frequently anxious, they will be hesitant and unsure about trying new things. As children grow and come into contact with friends, teachers and other outsiders, they continuously reassess their self-esteem and pass many stages of self-doubt. As parents, we can help to build their self-confidence by giving them the skills to think more positively. The best way to do this is to model a positive attitude.

Here are some more thoughts on why you should think positively.

- Employed mothers feel guilty largely because we base our lifestyle expectations on the experiences of the last generation. The world is different from 30 years ago. We are actually agents of change because we have moved on from the past but not yet arrived at a point where mothers working outside the home are the norm. We feel guilty because we get mixed messages about working outside and there are very few role models. So think of yourself not as an inadequate or self-centred mother but as one who, along with other working mothers, is creating a new paradigm for raising children; a paradigm based on fulfilment for the mother as well as active nurturing for her children.
- Recent studies show that, all other things being equal, children with working mothers perform equally well in social and academic areas as those whose mothers stay at home.
- Besides economic gain, your work gives you a personal identity,

intellectual stimulation and social interaction.

• Children value the increased self-esteem and status that work brings their mothers.

• You are delegating the more routine parts of childcare so that you can spend fun and creative time with your kids: the things they will remember.

There are enough reasons to be positive about your life. Being positive does not mean you need to bully yourself by living up to statements like "I can do this" or "I must do this", but means you should be optimistic about doing the best you can for your family each day. If you are positive, and see your glass as half full and not half empty, then you will consider praising the good things your child does more than complaining about the bad, and you will encourage your child's hopes rather than suppress them. In doing so, you foster a child who will not be intimidated by circumstances but will have a positive attitude important for future success and happiness in life.